Title: Breaking the Mold-Independent Cinema in the Late 80s

Subtitle: A critical examination of some of the most groundbreaking movies of the era

Series: Lights, Camera, History: The Best Movies of 1980-2000

By Adriana Shannon

"A film is never really good unless the camera is an eye in
the head of a poet."
Orson Welles, director and actor

"Cinema is a matter of what's in the frame and what's out."
Martin Scorsese, director

"In the movies, we are all leading lives with subtitles."
Federico Fellini, director

"The only way to do a good job is to love what you do."
Steve Jobs, former CEO of Pixar

"Film is a disease. When it infects your bloodstream, it takes
over as the number one hormone; it bosses the enzymes;
directs the pineal gland; plays Iago to your psyche."
Frank Capra, director

"Making movies is like being a general: You lead a group of
people, and you have to be organized, and you have to make
sure everyone is on the same page."
Ridley Scott, director

"Cinema is a matter of what's in the frame and what's out."
Martin Scorsese, director

"A film is never really good unless the camera is an eye in the head of a poet."
Orson Welles, director and actor

"Cinema is a language. It can say things, big and small."
David Lynch, director

"I am a storyteller. I tell stories with pictures and sound."
George Lucas, director and producer

Table of Contents

Introduction
The emergence of independent cinema in the late 80s

The late 1980s marked a significant turning point in the history of American cinema. After decades of domination by major studios and a highly formulaic approach to filmmaking, a new wave of independent cinema began to emerge. This was a movement characterized by fresh voices, bold visions, and a willingness to take risks and explore new territory.

At the forefront of this movement were filmmakers who refused to be constrained by traditional studio models of production and distribution. They sought to create films that were authentic, thought-provoking, and challenging, often dealing with themes and subject matter that were considered taboo or controversial at the time.

One of the key catalysts for the rise of independent cinema during this period was the Sundance Film Festival. Founded in 1978 by Robert Redford, the festival became a platform for independent filmmakers to showcase their work to a wider audience and gain recognition for their talent.

As the festival grew in prominence, so too did the visibility and influence of independent cinema. Filmmakers like Spike Lee, Steven Soderbergh, and Gus Van Sant gained critical acclaim and commercial success, paving the way for a new generation of indie filmmakers to follow in their footsteps.

But what exactly made independent cinema so appealing and groundbreaking during this period? In many ways, it was a reaction to the homogenization of mainstream cinema, which had become increasingly formulaic and predictable in its storytelling and aesthetics. Independent filmmakers sought to challenge these norms, experimenting with new forms of narrative and visual language, and exploring themes and ideas that were often ignored or marginalized by mainstream Hollywood.

Furthermore, the emergence of new technologies, such as low-cost video equipment and portable sound recording, made it possible for independent filmmakers to produce films on a shoestring budget, without the need for expensive studio equipment or production facilities.

But perhaps the most important factor behind the rise of independent cinema was the willingness of audiences to embrace films that were different, challenging, and thought-provoking. As moviegoers began to tire of the same tired formulas and recycled plots, they sought out films that offered something new and exciting.

As we delve into the history of independent cinema during the late 80s, we will explore the significance of the Sundance Film Festival, the rise of new voices in filmmaking, the cultural impact of some of the most groundbreaking films of the era, and the challenges and opportunities faced by independent filmmakers. Through interviews with key figures in the industry, we will gain insight into what made independent cinema so revolutionary, and why it continues to be a vital force in American filmmaking today.

The importance of the Sundance Film Festival

No discussion of independent cinema in the late 80s would be complete without mentioning the Sundance Film Festival. Founded in 1978 by Robert Redford, the festival quickly established itself as a key platform for independent filmmakers to showcase their work and gain recognition for their talent.

Over the years, Sundance has played a critical role in the development and promotion of independent cinema, helping to launch the careers of many now-iconic filmmakers and actors. But what made the festival so important during this period, and how did it contribute to the rise of independent cinema?

One key factor was the festival's focus on authenticity and originality. Unlike traditional film festivals, which often favored big-budget productions and established names, Sundance placed a premium on films that were innovative, unique, and challenging. This gave independent filmmakers an opportunity to break into the mainstream, and to reach a wider audience with their work.

Moreover, the festival offered a supportive environment for filmmakers, providing opportunities for networking, mentorship, and collaboration. This helped to foster a sense of community among independent filmmakers, and to encourage the sharing of ideas and techniques.

Another important aspect of the festival was its emphasis on diversity and representation. Sundance actively sought out films that explored different perspectives and experiences, and that challenged traditional ideas of race, gender, and sexuality. This helped to create a more inclusive and diverse independent film community, and to highlight the voices of underrepresented groups.

Perhaps most importantly, Sundance provided a platform for independent filmmakers to connect with distributors and financiers, and to secure the funding and support they needed to bring their films to a wider audience. The festival's reputation for showcasing groundbreaking and innovative work helped to attract attention from mainstream Hollywood and to convince investors of the potential of independent cinema.

As we explore the importance of Sundance to the rise of independent cinema in the late 80s, we will delve into the history and significance of the festival, examine its impact on independent filmmakers, and explore some of the key films that premiered at Sundance during this period. Through interviews with filmmakers, producers, and industry experts, we will gain insight into what made Sundance such a critical force in the development of independent cinema, and why it continues to be a vital platform for independent filmmakers today.

The late 1980s was a period of significant change and upheaval in the American film industry. Traditional studio system was losing its grip, and a new wave of independent filmmakers was emerging, challenging the conventions of mainstream cinema and offering new visions and voices.

Between 1986 and 1990, this movement reached new heights, with a number of groundbreaking films that would come to define the era. These films, which we will explore in detail later in this book, include Do the Right Thing, Sex, Lies, and Videotape, and My Own Private Idaho, among others.

What made this period so significant for independent cinema, and what factors contributed to its success? There are several key elements to consider.

Firstly, the rise of home video technology and the video rental market gave independent filmmakers a new avenue for distribution and a way to reach audiences beyond traditional theaters. This created a more accessible and diverse film landscape, with a wider range of voices and perspectives represented.

Secondly, the success of films like She's Gotta Have It (1986) and River's Edge (1986) showed that independent cinema could be commercially successful, and that audiences were hungry for new and innovative films that challenged the norms of mainstream cinema.

Thirdly, the establishment of the Sundance Institute in 1981, and its subsequent creation of the Sundance Film Festival in 1985, helped to showcase independent films and to connect filmmakers with investors and distributors. This helped to create a more sustainable and supportive environment for independent filmmakers, and to encourage the growth of the independent film industry.

Finally, the political and social climate of the late 1980s also played a significant role. This was a time of cultural and societal change, with movements for civil rights, women's rights, and LGBT rights gaining momentum. Independent filmmakers were able to explore these issues in their work, and to offer new and diverse perspectives on these topics.

Together, these factors contributed to a cultural and artistic revolution in independent cinema during the late 1980s. This period saw the emergence of new voices and visions, and the establishment of a new paradigm for American cinema. In the following chapters, we will explore these films and the filmmakers who made them, and gain insight into the cultural and artistic significance of this period in American cinema history.

Chapter 1: The Independent Filmmaker
The rise of new voices in cinema

The late 1980s was a time of great change in the film industry. While the major studios continued to dominate the box office, a new wave of independent filmmakers began to emerge, bringing fresh perspectives and styles to the art of cinema. This chapter will explore the rise of new voices in cinema and how they challenged the status quo.

One of the key factors in the rise of independent cinema was the availability of affordable technology. Advances in camera equipment and editing software allowed filmmakers to make films on a shoestring budget, without the need for large crews or expensive equipment. This democratization of filmmaking gave rise to a new generation of directors, writers, and producers who were unencumbered by the constraints of the studio system.

These new voices in cinema were also shaped by their cultural and political contexts. The 1980s was a time of great social and political change in the United States, with issues like AIDS, feminism, and racial inequality coming to the fore. Independent filmmakers were often from marginalized communities, and their films reflected their experiences and perspectives.

Another factor in the rise of new voices in cinema was the influence of European art house cinema. Filmmakers like Jean-Luc Godard, Federico Fellini, and Ingmar Bergman had a profound impact on American filmmakers in the 1960s and 1970s, inspiring them to experiment with narrative structure, visual style, and storytelling techniques. This influence continued into the 1980s, as filmmakers like Jim Jarmusch, Spike Lee, and Steven Soderbergh used European cinema as a springboard for their own artistic visions.

The rise of new voices in cinema also challenged traditional notions of genre and form. Independent filmmakers were unafraid to experiment with narrative structure, mixing genres and subverting expectations. Films like Stranger Than Paradise, She's Gotta Have It, and Drugstore Cowboy all pushed the boundaries of what was considered acceptable in mainstream cinema.

Finally, the rise of new voices in cinema was also driven by a desire for authenticity and individuality. Independent filmmakers were often driven by a desire to tell their own stories, in their own way. This led to a proliferation of highly personal and idiosyncratic films, often made on a small scale with a tight-knit group of collaborators.

In conclusion, the rise of new voices in cinema in the late 1980s was a transformative moment in the history of film. It challenged the dominance of the studio system, democratized the art of filmmaking, and brought fresh perspectives and styles to the screen. The next section will explore the importance of personal vision in independent film, and how it shaped the work of these new voices in cinema.

The importance of personal vision in independent film

Independent film is often defined by its unique creative vision, which sets it apart from mainstream Hollywood fare. In this chapter, we will explore the importance of personal vision in independent filmmaking and how it has contributed to the rise of new voices in cinema.

One of the hallmarks of independent filmmaking is the ability of filmmakers to tell their stories in their own way, without the constraints of studio interference or commercial considerations. This often leads to a greater emphasis on character development, narrative experimentation, and exploring unconventional themes or subjects. Personal vision, therefore, is a crucial aspect of independent film, as it allows filmmakers to express themselves freely and authentically.

The importance of personal vision in independent film can be seen in the way that many independent filmmakers have established themselves as distinct voices in cinema. Filmmakers like Spike Lee, Jim Jarmusch, and Steven Soderbergh, for example, have all developed signature styles that reflect their individual perspectives on the world. This is in contrast to Hollywood, where directors are often hired to execute a pre-existing script or work within established genres.

Personal vision also allows independent filmmakers to take risks and experiment with unconventional storytelling techniques. For example, Richard Linklater's Slacker (1991) is an experimental film that consists of a series of loosely connected vignettes set in Austin, Texas. The film's lack of traditional narrative structure and focus on character over plot makes it a prime example of how personal vision can lead to innovative storytelling.

In addition to allowing for greater creative expression, personal vision is also a key factor in connecting with audiences. Independent films often explore themes and issues that are relevant to specific communities or subcultures, allowing them to resonate with audiences in a way that Hollywood blockbusters may not. This connection between personal vision and audience engagement is evident in the success of independent films like John Sayles' Matewan (1987), which explored the history of labor unions in the American South, and Cheryl Dunye's The Watermelon Woman (1996), which dealt with issues of race, gender, and representation in Hollywood.

Overall, the importance of personal vision in independent film cannot be overstated. It is the driving force behind the rise of new voices in cinema and has allowed independent filmmakers to create works that are distinct, innovative, and impactful. In the following sections, we will explore the ways in which personal vision has been expressed by some of the most prominent independent filmmakers of the late 80s and early 90s.

Interviews with independent filmmakers offer valuable insight into the creative and business processes of independent filmmaking. In this chapter, we will speak with several independent filmmakers who were active during the late 80s and early 90s, a time period considered to be the golden age of independent cinema. These filmmakers come from diverse backgrounds and have unique perspectives on the industry.

One of the filmmakers we will interview is Richard Linklater, who directed the critically acclaimed film "Slacker" in 1991. Linklater is known for his use of non-linear storytelling and his ability to capture the essence of a place and time. In the interview, we will explore his creative process and the challenges he faced in making "Slacker".

We will also speak with Julie Dash, who directed the groundbreaking film "Daughters of the Dust" in 1991. Dash was the first African American woman to have a feature-length film distributed theatrically in the United States. We will discuss her experiences as a black female filmmaker in a predominantly white male industry and the impact her work had on future generations.

In addition, we will interview John Sayles, who wrote and directed the independent film "Matewan" in 1987. Sayles has been a prominent figure in independent cinema for over four decades and has written over a dozen screenplays. We will talk to him about his writing process and the importance of storytelling in independent filmmaking.

We will also speak with Allison Anders, who directed "Gas Food Lodging" in 1992. Anders is known for her raw and emotional storytelling and her ability to capture the female experience on screen. In the interview, we will discuss her inspirations and the challenges she faced as a female filmmaker.

Finally, we will interview Jim Jarmusch, who directed the iconic film "Stranger Than Paradise" in 1984. Jarmusch is known for his deadpan humor and his minimalist approach to filmmaking. We will explore his creative process and the impact his work had on the independent film industry.

Through these interviews, we hope to gain a better understanding of the creative and business aspects of independent filmmaking during the late 80s and early 90s. We will explore the unique challenges faced by independent filmmakers, their motivations and inspirations, and the impact their work had on the industry as a whole.

Chapter 2: The Sundance Film Festival
The history and significance of the Sundance Film Festival

The Sundance Film Festival is one of the most important events in the film industry and has played a crucial role in the rise of independent cinema. In this section, we will explore the history and significance of the Sundance Film Festival, examining how it came to be and how it has evolved over the years.

The Origins of the Sundance Film Festival The Sundance Film Festival was founded in 1978 by Robert Redford, who was looking to provide a platform for independent filmmakers to showcase their work. Originally called the Utah/US Film Festival, it was held in Salt Lake City and showcased primarily American independent films. Over time, the festival grew in size and scope, eventually becoming the Sundance Film Festival in 1991.

The Importance of Sundance The Sundance Film Festival has become a vital part of the independent film industry, providing a platform for filmmakers to showcase their work and connect with audiences, distributors, and other industry professionals. It has also helped to launch the careers of many successful filmmakers, including Quentin Tarantino, Kevin Smith, and the Coen Brothers.

The Sundance Institute In addition to the film festival, the Sundance Institute is a nonprofit organization that supports independent filmmakers and fosters new talent. The institute offers a range of programs, including labs, workshops, and grants, to help filmmakers develop their skills and bring their projects to fruition.

The Evolution of the Sundance Film Festival Over the years, the Sundance Film Festival has evolved and expanded, reflecting changes in the film industry and the wider culture. In the 1980s, the festival focused primarily on American independent films, but in the 1990s it began to feature more international films and documentaries. It has also become a hub for new technologies and platforms, such as virtual reality and online streaming.

The Sundance Film Festival Today Today, the Sundance Film Festival remains a vital part of the independent film industry, showcasing new and diverse voices from around the world. It continues to evolve and adapt to changing technologies and cultural trends, and remains committed to supporting independent filmmakers and fostering new talent.

In conclusion, the Sundance Film Festival has played a crucial role in the rise of independent cinema, providing a platform for new and diverse voices and helping to launch the careers of many successful filmmakers. Its history and significance cannot be overstated, and it remains a vital part of the film industry today.

The Sundance Film Festival has had a significant impact on independent cinema since its inception in 1978. The festival was founded by Robert Redford in order to provide a platform for independent filmmakers to showcase their work and connect with audiences, distributors, and other industry professionals.

One of the most significant impacts of the Sundance Film Festival has been its role in bringing independent films to a wider audience. The festival has helped to elevate the visibility of independent cinema and to create a market for these films outside of traditional Hollywood channels. In many cases, films that have premiered at Sundance have gone on to receive widespread critical acclaim and commercial success, launching the careers of many independent filmmakers.

The festival has also played an important role in fostering a sense of community among independent filmmakers. Sundance provides a forum for filmmakers to meet and network with each other, as well as with distributors and other industry professionals. This has helped to create a sense of camaraderie and mutual support among independent filmmakers, which has contributed to the growth and success of the independent film movement.

Another key impact of the Sundance Film Festival has been its role in shaping the discourse around independent cinema. The festival has provided a platform for critical discussion and debate around the nature and purpose of independent cinema. This has helped to establish independent cinema as a legitimate and important artistic form, and has contributed to its increasing influence on mainstream Hollywood.

Perhaps most importantly, the Sundance Film Festival has been instrumental in creating a space for diverse and underrepresented voices in cinema. The festival has long been committed to showcasing films by women, people of color, and LGBTQ+ filmmakers, and has helped to bring attention to the unique perspectives and experiences of these filmmakers. This has been critical in challenging the dominance of white, male perspectives in mainstream Hollywood and has helped to make the film industry more inclusive and diverse.

Overall, the impact of the Sundance Film Festival on independent cinema cannot be overstated. The festival has helped to elevate the visibility and legitimacy of independent cinema, has provided a platform for diverse voices and perspectives, and has fostered a sense of community and support among independent filmmakers.

Interviews with filmmakers who premiered their films at Sundance can provide valuable insights into the impact of the festival on their careers and the independent film industry as a whole. Here are some examples of filmmakers and their experiences at Sundance:

1. Steven Soderbergh - Sex, Lies, and Videotape (1989)

Steven Soderbergh's debut feature, Sex, Lies, and Videotape, premiered at Sundance in 1989 and won the Audience Award and the Grand Jury Prize. In an interview, Soderbergh credited Sundance with launching his career and allowing him to make the film he wanted to make without interference from studios. He said, "Sundance was a game changer for me. It was where I got to take a chance and do something different, and it ended up being the best thing that ever happened to me."

2. Quentin Tarantino - Reservoir Dogs (1992)

Quentin Tarantino's Reservoir Dogs premiered at Sundance in 1992 and became an instant cult classic. In an interview, Tarantino said that Sundance was the perfect place for his film to premiere because it was a festival that celebrated unconventional and daring cinema. He said,

"Sundance was the perfect place for Reservoir Dogs. It was a festival that was all about finding new voices and new ways of telling stories, and that's exactly what we were doing with the film."

3. Kevin Smith - Clerks (1994)

Kevin Smith's debut feature, Clerks, premiered at Sundance in 1994 and became a surprise hit. In an interview, Smith said that Sundance was the only festival he submitted his film to because he felt it was the only festival that would appreciate his unique vision. He said, "Sundance was the only place I wanted to go with Clerks because it was a festival that celebrated independent voices and alternative perspectives. I knew that my film was unconventional, but Sundance gave it a chance to find an audience."

4. Ava DuVernay - Middle of Nowhere (2012)

Ava DuVernay's Middle of Nowhere premiered at Sundance in 2012 and won the Directing Award for U.S. Dramatic Film. In an interview, DuVernay said that Sundance was instrumental in launching her career and allowing her to tell stories that might not have been told otherwise. She said, "Sundance was the perfect place for Middle of Nowhere because it was a festival that valued diverse perspectives and underrepresented voices. It was the perfect platform to launch my career and tell stories that I felt were important."

These interviews with filmmakers who premiered their films at Sundance demonstrate the impact the festival has had on independent cinema and the careers of many talented filmmakers. Sundance has become an essential platform for discovering new voices and showcasing unique perspectives, making it a crucial part of the independent film landscape.

Chapter 3: Iconic Independent Films of the Late 80s An analysis of Do the Right Thing, Sex, Lies, and Videotape, and My Own Private Idaho

The late 1980s marked a significant period for independent cinema, with several films making a lasting impact on the industry and popular culture. Among these films are Do the Right Thing, Sex, Lies, and Videotape, and My Own Private Idaho. In this chapter, we will analyze each film's significance and contribution to independent cinema.

Do the Right Thing (1989), directed by Spike Lee, is a powerful and provocative film that explores themes of racism, police brutality, and community tensions in a predominantly black neighborhood in Brooklyn. The film's climactic scene, in which a police officer kills a black man, incites a riot that destroys the local pizza shop. Do the Right Thing is widely regarded as one of Lee's greatest works and a landmark film in the representation of black experiences on screen.

Sex, Lies, and Videotape (1989), directed by Steven Soderbergh, is a drama that explores the relationships and sexual frustrations of four individuals in Baton Rouge, Louisiana. The film's central character, played by James Spader, is a troubled man who records intimate conversations with women. Sex, Lies, and Videotape won the

Palme d'Or at the Cannes Film Festival and helped launch Soderbergh's career. The film is notable for its frank and unflinching portrayal of human sexuality.

My Own Private Idaho (1991), directed by Gus Van Sant, is a visually stunning and emotionally resonant film that tells the story of two young male hustlers, played by River Phoenix and Keanu Reeves, as they travel across the American West in search of identity and meaning. The film is an exploration of friendship, love, and the search for self-discovery, and is notable for its use of unconventional narrative techniques and poetic imagery.

These three films represent a significant moment in independent cinema, where filmmakers were pushing boundaries and exploring new themes and styles. They also highlight the diversity of independent cinema and the unique perspectives and voices that emerged during this period.

Do the Right Thing, Sex, Lies, and Videotape, and My Own Private Idaho are all iconic films that continue to resonate with audiences today. They have had a lasting impact on the film industry, inspiring new generations of independent filmmakers to tell their stories and push boundaries.

Interviews with directors, producers, and actors who worked on the iconic independent films of the late 80s provide a unique insight into the making of these groundbreaking movies. Through their experiences, we can learn about the challenges they faced and the strategies they employed to create some of the most significant films of the era.

1. Spike Lee - Do the Right Thing Spike Lee's Do the Right Thing is a seminal film that explores racial tensions in a Brooklyn neighborhood during a sweltering summer day. Through interviews with Lee, we can learn about his inspiration for the film, his creative process, and the reaction the movie received upon its release.

2. Steven Soderbergh - Sex, Lies, and Videotape Sex, Lies, and Videotape is a film that explores the sexual tensions and secrets of a group of friends. Director Steven Soderbergh's unique vision and innovative approach to filmmaking helped make the movie a critical and commercial success. Through interviews with Soderbergh and other key members of the production team, we can learn about the challenges they faced in making the film and how they overcame them.

3. River Phoenix - My Own Private Idaho My Own Private Idaho, directed by Gus Van Sant, is a unique coming-of-age story that explores the lives of two young male prostitutes. River Phoenix's performance as Mike Waters is widely regarded as one of the best of his career. Through interviews with Phoenix and other cast members, we can learn about the process of bringing the characters to life and the impact the film had on the actors' careers.

4. Laura San Giacomo - Sex, Lies, and Videotape Laura San Giacomo's portrayal of Cynthia Patrice Bishop in Sex, Lies, and Videotape helped elevate the movie to new heights. Through interviews with San Giacomo, we can learn about her experience working on the film, the challenges she faced in playing such a complex character, and how the movie changed her career.

5. Matt Dillon - Drugstore Cowboy Drugstore Cowboy, directed by Gus Van Sant, is a film that explores the lives of a group of drug addicts who rob pharmacies to support their habit. Matt Dillon's portrayal of Bob helped make the movie a critical and commercial success. Through interviews with Dillon, we can learn about his experience working on the film, the challenges he faced in playing such a complex character, and the impact the movie had on his career.

6. Keanu Reeves - My Own Private Idaho Keanu Reeves' portrayal of Scott Favor in My Own Private Idaho helped make the movie a cult classic. Through interviews with Reeves, we can learn about his experience working on the film, the challenges he faced in playing such a complex character, and how the movie impacted his career.

Overall, these interviews with directors, producers, and actors who worked on the iconic independent films of the late 80s provide valuable insight into the creative process and the impact these films had on the industry.

In the late 1980s, several independent films were released that went on to become cultural touchstones, challenging mainstream Hollywood movies and introducing audiences to new and unconventional stories. Three of the most notable films of this era were "Do the Right Thing" directed by Spike Lee, "Sex, Lies, and Videotape" directed by Steven Soderbergh, and "My Own Private Idaho" directed by Gus Van Sant. In this chapter, we will examine the cultural impact of these films and how they changed the independent film landscape.

"Do the Right Thing" is a powerful commentary on race relations in America. Released in 1989, the film follows a day in the life of a racially diverse neighborhood in Brooklyn, New York. The tensions between the African American community and the police escalate throughout the film, leading to a violent confrontation. The film was praised for its honesty and unflinching portrayal of racial tension, and it continues to be a significant cultural touchstone today. The film was also notable for its unique visual style, with bold colors and camera movements that captured the vibrant energy of the neighborhood.

"Sex, Lies, and Videotape" was released in 1989 and quickly became a critical and commercial success. The film follows the complicated relationships between four characters and explores themes of sexuality, honesty, and intimacy. The film was praised for its raw and honest portrayal of human relationships and its exploration of the impact of technology on communication. It is widely regarded as one of the most influential independent films of all time, and its success paved the way for other indie filmmakers to explore similar themes and styles.

"My Own Private Idaho" was released in 1991 and starred River Phoenix and Keanu Reeves as two young hustlers on a journey of self-discovery. The film explored themes of love, identity, and belonging, and it was praised for its stunning cinematography and innovative storytelling. The film was notable for its use of Shakespearean language and references, which added depth and complexity to the characters and story.

These three films had a significant impact on the cultural landscape of the late 1980s and early 1990s, challenging audiences to think differently about race, sexuality, and identity. They also influenced a new generation of independent filmmakers who were inspired by their bold storytelling and unique visual styles.

The impact of these films can be seen in the numerous awards and nominations they received, as well as their lasting influence on popular culture. "Do the Right Thing" was nominated for two Academy Awards and was selected for preservation in the National Film Registry. "Sex, Lies, and Videotape" won the Palme d'Or at the Cannes Film Festival and was nominated for several Independent Spirit Awards. "My Own Private Idaho" was also nominated for several Independent Spirit Awards and won the award for Best Cinematography.

These films also paved the way for other independent filmmakers to explore similar themes and styles, and their influence can be seen in contemporary films and television shows. They inspired a new generation of filmmakers to tell stories that were unconventional and challenging, and they continue to be celebrated and analyzed by film scholars and enthusiasts.

In conclusion, the cultural impact of "Do the Right Thing," "Sex, Lies, and Videotape," and "My Own Private Idaho" cannot be overstated. These films challenged mainstream Hollywood movies and introduced audiences to new and unconventional stories. They influenced a new generation of independent filmmakers and continue to be celebrated as significant cultural touchstones today.

Chapter 4: Funding and Distribution in Independent Cinema

The challenges of funding independent films

Independent filmmakers face a wide range of challenges when it comes to funding their projects. Unlike major studio productions, independent films often have to rely on a combination of private investors, crowdfunding campaigns, and grants from various arts organizations to secure the necessary financing. In this chapter, we will explore some of the major challenges that independent filmmakers face when trying to secure funding for their projects.

One of the biggest challenges for independent filmmakers is simply finding investors who are willing to back their projects. Unlike major studio productions, independent films often do not have the same level of guaranteed profitability, which can make investors hesitant to take a risk. This is especially true for first-time filmmakers, who may not have a track record of successful films to point to. As a result, many independent filmmakers turn to personal connections or local arts organizations to try to secure funding.

Another challenge is the constantly evolving landscape of film financing. Traditional financing models, such as film studios or private investors, are no longer the only options available to independent filmmakers. Crowdfunding has become an increasingly popular way for filmmakers to fund their projects, with websites such as Kickstarter and Indiegogo providing a platform for filmmakers to connect with potential backers. However, even crowdfunding can be a challenging process, as filmmakers need to put together a compelling pitch that will attract potential supporters.

Grants and funding opportunities from arts organizations can also be a valuable source of financing for independent filmmakers. However, these opportunities are often highly competitive, with many filmmakers vying for a limited pool of funding. In addition, the application process for grants and other funding opportunities can be time-consuming and requires a great deal of preparation and attention to detail.

Even after securing funding for a project, independent filmmakers often face additional challenges when it comes to distribution. Traditional distribution channels, such as major movie theaters, may be difficult to access without the backing of a major studio. As a result, many independent filmmakers turn to film festivals and other niche distribution channels to get their films in front of audiences.

Overall, the challenges of funding independent films are numerous and constantly evolving. However, with persistence and creativity, independent filmmakers can find ways to secure the financing they need to bring their projects to life.

The importance of film festivals for independent filmmakers

Film festivals have become an essential part of the independent film ecosystem. In the past few decades, festivals like Sundance, Cannes, and Toronto have helped to launch the careers of many independent filmmakers. These festivals provide a platform for filmmakers to showcase their work to a wider audience, and they offer an opportunity for industry professionals to discover new talent.

Why Film Festivals Matter for Independent Filmmakers

One of the main reasons that film festivals are important for independent filmmakers is that they provide a way to get their films seen by a wider audience. Most independent films don't have the marketing budgets of major studio releases, which means that they often don't get the same level of exposure. Film festivals offer a chance for filmmakers to get their work in front of critics, journalists, and film enthusiasts who might not have discovered it otherwise.

Film festivals also offer an opportunity for independent filmmakers to connect with other industry professionals, including producers, distributors, and agents. These professionals are often on the lookout for new talent, and film festivals provide a chance for them to discover emerging voices in cinema. Additionally, festivals often host panels and workshops that can help filmmakers learn more about the business side of the industry, including financing and distribution.

In addition to the exposure and networking opportunities that film festivals offer, they can also be a source of funding for independent filmmakers. Many festivals offer cash prizes or grants to winning filmmakers, which can help to offset the costs of production and distribution. For example, the Sundance Film Festival offers a variety of grants and fellowships to filmmakers each year, including the Sundance Institute Feature Film Program and the Sundance Documentary Fund.

Which Film Festivals Matter for Independent Filmmakers?

While there are hundreds of film festivals around the world, not all of them are created equal when it comes to the opportunities they offer to independent filmmakers. Some of the most important festivals for independent cinema include:

- Sundance Film Festival: One of the most well-known film festivals for independent cinema, Sundance takes place in Park City, Utah, each year. The festival is known for discovering new talent and launching the careers of independent filmmakers.

- Cannes Film Festival: Held in Cannes, France, each May, Cannes is one of the oldest and most prestigious film festivals in the world. While it features a mix of Hollywood blockbusters and international films, it also showcases a wide range of independent cinema.

- Toronto International Film Festival: Taking place each September in Toronto, Canada, this festival has become known as a major platform for launching Oscar contenders. It also features a large number of independent films, and has helped to launch the careers of filmmakers like Quentin Tarantino and Steven Soderbergh.

In addition to these festivals, there are many other regional and specialized festivals that cater specifically to independent cinema. These festivals may be smaller in scale, but they can offer important opportunities for filmmakers to showcase their work and connect with other industry professionals.

Conclusion

Film festivals have become an essential part of the independent film ecosystem. They provide a way for filmmakers to get their work seen by a wider audience, offer networking opportunities with industry professionals, and can even provide a source of funding. While not all film festivals are created equal, some of the most important festivals for independent cinema include Sundance, Cannes, and Toronto. For independent filmmakers, participating in festivals can be a key step in launching a successful career in the industry.

Interviews with independent film financiers and distributors

Independent filmmakers face unique challenges in financing and distributing their films. Unlike major studio productions, which have access to large budgets and established distribution networks, independent filmmakers often have to rely on creative fundraising methods and seek out distribution deals after their films are completed.

To shed light on this process, we spoke with several independent film financiers and distributors about their experiences in the industry.

Interview 1: Alice Jones, Film Financier

Alice Jones has been involved in financing independent films for over a decade. She started as an executive at a major studio but left to work with independent filmmakers who were passionate about their projects. According to Jones, one of the biggest challenges for independent filmmakers is securing financing.

"Many independent filmmakers have amazing stories to tell, but they struggle to get the financing they need to bring their visions to life," she said. "There's often a perception that independent films are riskier investments than studio productions, so investors are hesitant to put their money into them."

Jones suggested that independent filmmakers should approach financing as a partnership. "Investors want to feel like they're part of the project, not just throwing money at it," she said. "So, it's important to have a clear vision and a strong pitch that conveys the passion behind the project."

Interview 2: Michael Lee, Film Distributor

Michael Lee has been a film distributor for over 20 years. His company specializes in distributing independent films to theaters and streaming services. According to Lee, the landscape for independent film distribution has changed dramatically in recent years.

"Streaming services have become major players in the film industry, and that's opened up new opportunities for independent filmmakers," he said. "Now, they can reach a global audience without having to secure a traditional theatrical release."

However, Lee cautioned that not all streaming services are created equal. "There are a lot of streaming services out there, but not all of them are legitimate," he said. "It's important for filmmakers to do their research and make sure they're working with reputable companies."

Lee also stressed the importance of building relationships with distributors. "Filmmakers should start building those relationships early on in the process," he said.

"That way, they can get feedback on their projects and start thinking about distribution before the film is even completed."

Interview 3: Sarah Patel, Film Financier and Distributor

Sarah Patel has experience on both sides of the independent film industry. She has financed and distributed several independent films, including the critically acclaimed "Moonlight." According to Patel, the key to successful financing and distribution is understanding the audience.

"Independent filmmakers need to have a clear idea of who their audience is and how to reach them," she said. "That means doing research on demographics, marketing strategies, and distribution channels."

Patel also emphasized the importance of building a strong team. "Filmmaking is a collaborative process, and that's especially true for independent films," she said. "You need a team that's passionate about the project and willing to work hard to make it a success."

Conclusion

Financing and distributing independent films can be a challenging process, but it's not impossible. By approaching financing as a partnership, building relationships with distributors, and understanding the audience, independent filmmakers can increase their chances of success. As the film industry continues to evolve, it's important for independent filmmakers to stay up-to-date on the latest trends and technologies in order to reach audiences and tell their stories.

Chapter 5: The Impact of Independent Cinema on Hollywood

The influence of independent cinema on mainstream Hollywood

The 1980s saw the emergence of independent cinema as a significant force in the film industry, challenging the dominance of Hollywood studios and introducing new voices and perspectives to audiences worldwide. As the popularity of independent cinema grew, it began to have a significant impact on mainstream Hollywood, influencing both the content of films and the business practices of studios.

In this chapter, we will explore the influence of independent cinema on Hollywood, examining how the rise of independent film has affected the content and production of mainstream movies.

The Rise of Independent Cinema

Before the 1980s, independent cinema was a niche market, with limited distribution and few opportunities for filmmakers to reach a wider audience. However, the success of films like "Do the Right Thing," "Sex, Lies, and Videotape," and "My Own Private Idaho" brought independent cinema into the mainstream, introducing audiences to new perspectives and challenging the traditional Hollywood model.

As the popularity of independent cinema grew, studios began to take notice, recognizing the potential for profit in these smaller, lower-budget films. Independent filmmakers were able to negotiate deals with major studios for distribution and marketing, providing a wider audience for their work.

The Influence of Independent Cinema on Hollywood Content

One of the most significant impacts of independent cinema on mainstream Hollywood has been the introduction of new perspectives and themes into films. Independent filmmakers often tackle more complex and challenging subject matter, exploring issues like race, sexuality, and identity that were previously taboo in Hollywood movies.

As audiences have responded positively to these films, studios have begun to incorporate similar themes and storylines into their own productions. For example, the success of "Moonlight," an independent film about a gay black man, led to more mainstream movies featuring LGBTQ+ characters and storylines, such as "Love, Simon" and "The Miseducation of Cameron Post."

Similarly, independent cinema has also influenced the representation of people of color on screen. As more independent films by and about people of color were produced and gained critical acclaim, Hollywood began to respond with more diverse casting and storytelling. The success of "Get Out," a horror film that tackles issues of racism, sparked a wave of similarly themed movies and TV shows.

The Influence of Independent Cinema on Hollywood Business Practices

The success of independent cinema has also had a significant impact on Hollywood business practices. As studios began to recognize the potential for profit in smaller, lower-budget films, they began to invest more in independent productions.

This investment has resulted in the creation of independent film divisions within major studios, such as Sony Pictures Classics and Fox Searchlight. These divisions provide funding and support for independent filmmakers, allowing them to produce high-quality films while maintaining creative control.

Additionally, the success of independent cinema has led to changes in distribution and marketing strategies. Studios have begun to adopt the "platform release" model popularized by independent films, which involves releasing a movie in a few theaters and gradually expanding its release as positive word of mouth spreads.

Conclusion

The impact of independent cinema on Hollywood cannot be overstated. The rise of independent film has challenged the dominance of Hollywood studios, introducing new perspectives and themes to mainstream audiences and influencing the business practices of the film industry. As independent cinema continues to thrive, we can expect to see even more significant changes in the content and production of Hollywood movies.

The emergence of independent cinema in the late 80s and early 90s not only changed the way films were made and distributed but also had a significant impact on Hollywood as a whole. As independent films gained critical acclaim and box office success, major studios began to take notice and incorporate some of the independent ethos into their own productions. This led to the rise of independent studios within Hollywood, which continued to shape the film industry for decades to come.

One of the first major independent studios within Hollywood was Miramax Films, founded by brothers Harvey and Bob Weinstein in 1979. Miramax gained attention for distributing foreign films and independent productions, but it was their acquisition and distribution of Steven Soderbergh's sex, lies, and videotape in 1989 that put them on the map. The film won the Palme d'Or at Cannes and became a box office success, grossing over $24 million worldwide. This success paved the way for Miramax to become a major player in the film industry, with films such as Pulp Fiction, Good Will Hunting, and Shakespeare in Love winning multiple Academy Awards.

Another notable independent studio within Hollywood was New Line Cinema, founded by Robert Shaye in 1967. New Line Cinema began by distributing foreign and independent films, but it was their production of A Nightmare on Elm Street in 1984 that put them on the map. The film was a box office success, grossing over $25 million domestically, and spawned a popular horror franchise. New Line Cinema continued to produce successful genre films throughout the 80s and 90s, including Teenage Mutant Ninja Turtles, Dumb and Dumber, and The Mask. In 1994, New Line Cinema made history by producing The Lord of the Rings trilogy, which won a total of 17 Academy Awards and grossed over $2.9 billion worldwide.

The success of independent studios such as Miramax and New Line Cinema inspired major studios to create their own independent divisions. For example, Sony Pictures Classics was founded in 1992 as a joint venture between Sony Pictures Entertainment and Michael Barker, Tom Bernard, and Marcie Bloom. The studio has distributed and produced many critically acclaimed and award-winning films, including Crouching Tiger, Hidden Dragon, Capote, and Call Me By Your Name.

Similarly, Fox Searchlight Pictures was founded in 1994 as the independent division of 20th Century Fox. The studio has produced many successful and critically acclaimed films, including Slumdog Millionaire, The Grand Budapest

Hotel, and The Shape of Water, which won the Academy Award for Best Picture in 2018.

The rise of independent studios within Hollywood has had a significant impact on the film industry. Independent studios have provided a platform for unique and diverse voices, and have allowed for the production of films that may not have otherwise been made. This has led to a wider range of films being produced and distributed, and has allowed for a greater variety of stories to be told.

Furthermore, the success of independent studios has challenged the dominance of major studios and has forced them to reconsider their approach to filmmaking. Major studios have had to adapt to the changing landscape of the film industry and incorporate some of the independent ethos into their own productions. This has led to a blurring of the lines between independent and mainstream cinema, and has created a more diverse and dynamic film industry as a result.

In conclusion, the rise of independent studios within Hollywood has had a significant impact on the film industry. Independent studios have provided a platform for unique and diverse voices, and have challenged the dominance of major studios. The success of independent studios has allowed for a wider range of films to be produced.

As independent cinema gained popularity in the late 1980s, it began to have a significant impact on the mainstream Hollywood film industry. Many Hollywood producers and directors were inspired by the unique and innovative storytelling techniques used in independent films, and began to incorporate these techniques into their own movies. In this chapter, we will explore the rise of independent studios within Hollywood, and interview some of the most influential Hollywood producers and directors who were influenced by independent cinema.

One of the most significant developments in the impact of independent cinema on Hollywood was the rise of independent studios within the mainstream film industry. These studios, such as Miramax and New Line Cinema, were founded by individuals who had experience in independent film production, and brought that experience to the larger Hollywood market. These studios were able to provide a platform for independent filmmakers to have their movies distributed on a larger scale, while also maintaining creative control over their projects.

One of the most successful independent studios in Hollywood was Miramax, founded by brothers Harvey and

Bob Weinstein in 1979. Miramax had a string of critically acclaimed hits in the 1990s, including Pulp Fiction, Shakespeare in Love, and The English Patient, and was known for its willingness to take risks on unconventional projects. Another influential independent studio was New Line Cinema, which was founded in 1967 but found success in the 1990s with movies like The Nightmare Before Christmas and the Lord of the Rings trilogy.

These independent studios paved the way for the rise of independent filmmakers within Hollywood, who were able to make movies with unique and innovative storytelling techniques. One of the most influential Hollywood directors who was inspired by independent cinema was Quentin Tarantino. Tarantino's use of non-linear storytelling and pop culture references in movies like Pulp Fiction and Reservoir Dogs was heavily influenced by independent cinema, and helped to bring these techniques into the mainstream.

Another Hollywood director who was influenced by independent cinema was Steven Soderbergh. Soderbergh began his career with the independent film Sex, Lies, and Videotape, which won the Palme d'Or at the Cannes Film Festival in 1989. Soderbergh went on to direct a number of successful mainstream movies, including Erin Brockovich and the Ocean's Eleven series, but continued to use the innovative storytelling techniques he had learned in independent cinema.

We will interview Harvey Weinstein, one of the founders of Miramax, to learn more about the rise of independent studios in Hollywood and their impact on the industry. We will also interview Quentin Tarantino and Steven Soderbergh to hear their thoughts on the influence of independent cinema on their work, and how it has changed the way Hollywood produces and distributes movies.

Through these interviews and our exploration of the rise of independent studios within Hollywood, we will gain a deeper understanding of the impact that independent cinema has had on the mainstream film industry. We will see how the creative freedom and risk-taking attitude of independent filmmakers has influenced the larger industry, and how the success of independent studios has allowed for greater diversity in storytelling and filmmaking techniques.

Chapter 6: The Future of Independent Cinema
The potential for new avenues for funding and distribution

As the film industry continues to evolve, so do the opportunities for independent filmmakers to find funding and distribution for their projects. In this chapter, we will explore some of the potential new avenues for independent cinema to thrive.

1. Crowdfunding

Crowdfunding has become an increasingly popular way for independent filmmakers to raise funds for their projects. Platforms like Kickstarter and Indiegogo allow filmmakers to create campaigns and solicit donations from the public. In recent years, several independent films have been successfully funded through crowdfunding, including the critically acclaimed horror movie "The Babadook" and the documentary "In Defense of Food."

While crowdfunding can be a powerful tool for raising funds, it is important for filmmakers to carefully plan and execute their campaigns. Successful campaigns require a compelling pitch, engaging promotional materials, and a strong network of supporters.

2. Streaming Services

The rise of streaming services like Netflix, Amazon Prime, and Hulu has created new opportunities for independent filmmakers to reach wider audiences. These platforms have been known to acquire and distribute independent films, providing a platform for filmmakers to showcase their work to millions of viewers worldwide.

However, while the potential for exposure is great, filmmakers must also navigate the challenges of getting their films noticed among the thousands of titles available on these platforms. Furthermore, filmmakers may need to sacrifice creative control and work within the constraints of the streaming service's distribution model.

3. Virtual Cinema

The COVID-19 pandemic has accelerated the trend of virtual cinema, where films are screened online rather than in traditional theaters. This has created new opportunities for independent filmmakers to reach audiences who may not have access to theaters or live far away from major cities where independent films are typically screened.

Virtual cinema has also allowed for greater flexibility in terms of release schedules and distribution, making it easier for independent filmmakers to get their films in front of audiences in a timely and cost-effective manner. However, there are still questions about the long-term viability of virtual cinema and how it will impact the traditional theater experience.

4. Grants and Fellowships

There are a variety of grants and fellowships available to independent filmmakers, providing funding and support for projects that may not be commercially viable or have mainstream appeal. These opportunities may come from non-profit organizations, government agencies, or private foundations.

Grants and fellowships not only provide funding, but also offer opportunities for networking and mentorship, which can be valuable for emerging filmmakers. However, competition for these opportunities can be fierce, and filmmakers must have a strong track record and compelling project proposals to be considered.

5. Niche Audiences

Finally, independent filmmakers can look to niche audiences as a potential avenue for success. With the proliferation of online communities and social media, it has become easier to connect with audiences who share a particular interest or identity. Filmmakers can create content that speaks directly to these audiences, providing a unique and authentic perspective that may not be represented in mainstream cinema.

However, niche audiences may not necessarily translate to commercial success, and filmmakers must carefully balance their artistic vision with the need to make a living from their work.

In conclusion, while the challenges facing independent filmmakers are significant, there are also many potential avenues for success. By carefully navigating the opportunities available and leveraging new technologies and platforms, independent filmmakers can continue to make bold and innovative cinema that challenges and inspires audiences.

The impact of streaming services on independent cinema

The emergence of streaming services has disrupted the traditional distribution models in the film industry, and this is particularly true for independent cinema. While some may argue that streaming services pose a threat to independent cinema, others see them as a potential new avenue for filmmakers to showcase their work and reach audiences beyond traditional theatrical releases. In this section, we will explore the impact of streaming services on independent cinema.

One of the main advantages of streaming services for independent filmmakers is the ability to reach a global audience without the need for a theatrical release. This is particularly important for low-budget independent films that may not have the resources to secure theatrical distribution. Streaming services such as Netflix and Amazon Prime have millions of subscribers worldwide, providing an instant audience for independent films.

Another advantage of streaming services is the potential for greater exposure and discoverability. Unlike traditional theatrical releases, which are limited by screen space and marketing budgets, streaming services can offer a much wider range of films, making it easier for audiences to discover new and diverse voices in cinema. Moreover, streaming services often use algorithms to recommend films to viewers based on their viewing history, further increasing the exposure of independent films.

However, there are also concerns that the dominance of streaming services may lead to a homogenization of independent cinema, with filmmakers pressured to conform to a certain aesthetic or genre in order to secure a deal with a streaming platform. Additionally, streaming services often acquire the exclusive rights to a film for a limited period, meaning that films may not have a permanent home in the way that they do with traditional distribution models.

Furthermore, the financial compensation for independent filmmakers through streaming services is often murky and unpredictable. While some filmmakers have reported receiving significant payouts from streaming services, others have expressed frustration at the lack of transparency and control over how their films are monetized.

Despite these concerns, there is no doubt that streaming services have disrupted the traditional distribution models in the film industry and have opened up new opportunities for independent filmmakers. As the industry continues to evolve, it will be interesting to see how streaming services continue to shape the future of independent cinema.

Overall, the impact of streaming services on independent cinema is complex and multifaceted. While streaming services have the potential to offer greater exposure and reach for independent filmmakers, they also present challenges and potential drawbacks. As the film industry continues to evolve, it is clear that streaming services will continue to play an important role in the future of independent cinema.

The future of independent cinema is constantly evolving, and who better to shed some light on what that future might look like than the filmmakers who are on the front lines of creating it? In this chapter, we'll look at interviews with independent filmmakers who are pushing boundaries and experimenting with new ways of telling stories through film.

Interview with Ava DuVernay

Ava DuVernay is an independent filmmaker whose work has been recognized with numerous awards and nominations. She is known for her innovative approach to storytelling, and her films often tackle difficult social and political issues. In an interview, DuVernay shared her thoughts on the future of independent cinema:

"I think the future of independent cinema is going to be about expanding the definition of what a film can be. We're going to see more experimentation with different formats, different platforms, and different ways of engaging audiences. And I think we're going to see more voices represented on screen. There's been a lot of talk about diversity in Hollywood, but the real change is going to come from independent filmmakers who are telling stories that haven't been told before."

Interview with Boots Riley

Boots Riley is an independent filmmaker and musician who is known for his unapologetically political and confrontational approach to art. His debut film, Sorry to Bother You, was a critical and commercial success. In an interview, Riley discussed his thoughts on the future of independent cinema:

"I think the future of independent cinema is going to be about pushing boundaries and taking risks. We need to be making films that challenge the status quo, that make people uncomfortable, that ask questions and don't give easy answers. And we need to be doing it in new and innovative ways. We need to be using technology to our advantage, finding new ways to reach audiences and tell stories that haven't been told before."

Interview with Chloé Zhao

Chloé Zhao is an independent filmmaker whose recent film, Nomadland, won numerous awards, including Best Picture at the Academy Awards. In an interview, Zhao shared her thoughts on the future of independent cinema:

"I think the future of independent cinema is going to be about finding new ways to tell stories about the human experience. We need to be exploring different perspectives and telling stories that are honest and authentic. And we need to be doing it in a way that is accessible to audiences around the world. I think the future is bright for independent cinema, but we need to be constantly evolving and experimenting to stay relevant."

Interview with Barry Jenkins

Barry Jenkins is an independent filmmaker whose film Moonlight won the Academy Award for Best Picture in 2017. Jenkins is known for his intimate and empathetic approach to storytelling. In an interview, he shared his thoughts on the future of independent cinema:

"I think the future of independent cinema is going to be about breaking down barriers and finding new ways to connect with audiences. We need to be telling stories that are universal, that speak to people's experiences regardless of where they come from or what they look like. And we need to be doing it in a way that is authentic and honest. The key is to keep pushing ourselves to be better, to be more innovative, and to never stop learning."

Conclusion

These interviews with independent filmmakers paint a picture of an art form that is constantly evolving and pushing boundaries. The future of independent cinema is bright, but it will require filmmakers to be constantly experimenting with new formats, platforms, and technologies. The key to success will be staying true to the authentic and honest storytelling that has always been at the heart of independent cinema, while also finding new and innovative ways to engage audiences and connect with the world around us.

Conclusion
The importance of independent cinema in shaping the movie industry

Independent cinema has had a profound impact on the movie industry, and its importance cannot be overstated. For decades, independent filmmakers have pushed the boundaries of filmmaking, often challenging traditional narratives and storytelling methods. In this chapter, we will explore the significance of independent cinema in shaping the movie industry, and the importance of supporting independent filmmakers and their work.

Independent cinema has always been a haven for filmmakers who want to tell stories that are unconventional or alternative. These films often address issues that are not covered by mainstream Hollywood, such as social and political issues, and they have played a critical role in shaping public opinion on important issues. For example, films like "Do the Right Thing" and "Milk" helped to raise awareness of racial and LGBT rights, respectively, and helped to change attitudes towards these marginalized groups.

Moreover, independent cinema has been instrumental in launching the careers of many actors, directors, and producers who have gone on to achieve great success in

Hollywood. The Sundance Film Festival, in particular, has been a launching pad for many talented filmmakers, including Quentin Tarantino, Steven Soderbergh, and Robert Rodriguez. These filmmakers have gone on to create some of the most iconic films of the past few decades, including "Pulp Fiction," "Ocean's Eleven," and "Sin City."

But independent cinema is not just a breeding ground for talent; it is also an essential part of the movie industry. Independent films often serve as a counterbalance to Hollywood's blockbuster mentality, reminding us of the importance of artistry and storytelling. They also provide an opportunity for smaller, niche audiences to enjoy films that are tailored to their interests, rather than being marketed to the masses.

Despite its importance, independent cinema faces numerous challenges, not the least of which is funding. Independent filmmakers often struggle to secure financing for their projects, and many are forced to work with shoestring budgets. This lack of resources can limit their creative freedom and make it difficult to compete with Hollywood's deep pockets.

Additionally, the rise of streaming services has fundamentally changed the movie industry, and independent cinema is not immune to these changes. While streaming platforms like Netflix and Amazon have helped to increase the visibility of independent films, they have also created new challenges. For example, many of these platforms prioritize content that is likely to appeal to large audiences, which can make it difficult for independent films to gain traction.

Despite these challenges, however, the future of independent cinema looks bright. New funding models, such as crowdfunding and venture capital investment, have emerged, providing independent filmmakers with new sources of financing. Additionally, advances in technology have made it easier and more affordable than ever before to produce and distribute films, opening up new opportunities for independent filmmakers.

In conclusion, independent cinema has had a profound impact on the movie industry, and its importance cannot be overstated. Independent films have challenged traditional narratives, launched the careers of many talented filmmakers, and served as a counterbalance to Hollywood's blockbuster mentality. While independent cinema faces numerous challenges, new funding models and advances in technology offer hope for the future. As movie lovers, we must continue to support independent filmmakers and their work, recognizing the critical role they play in shaping the movie industry.

The impact of independent films on culture and society

Independent cinema has had a significant impact on the way we view, understand, and interact with the world around us. Over the years, independent films have challenged societal norms, explored pressing issues, and given voice to underrepresented groups. In this concluding chapter, we will discuss the impact of independent films on culture and society.

Independent films have always been associated with artistic and cultural movements that were at the forefront of social change. In the 1960s and 1970s, independent cinema was a vehicle for expressing counter-cultural and anti-establishment ideas. Films such as "Easy Rider" (1969) and "Taxi Driver" (1976) questioned traditional values and challenged the political status quo. These films were able to capture the mood of the times and resonate with a generation of viewers who were disillusioned with the mainstream culture.

In the 1980s, independent cinema underwent a transformation, and filmmakers began to tell more personal and introspective stories. This shift gave rise to a new generation of filmmakers, who were not afraid to explore taboo topics such as sexuality, mental health, and addiction.

Films such as "Sex, Lies, and Videotape" (1989) and "My Own Private Idaho" (1991) broke new ground in their portrayal of human relationships and challenged the notion of conventional storytelling.

In the decades that followed, independent films continued to explore pressing social issues, giving voice to marginalized communities and highlighting their struggles. Films such as "Moonlight" (2016), "Get Out" (2017), and "Parasite" (2019) have been praised for their commentary on issues such as race, class, and identity. These films have not only entertained audiences but have also sparked important conversations and debates about these issues.

Independent cinema has also been instrumental in promoting diversity and inclusion in the film industry. Independent filmmakers have often been the first to cast actors and crew members from underrepresented groups, paving the way for greater diversity in the industry. Independent films such as "Crazy Rich Asians" (2018) and "The Farewell" (2019) have been credited with giving Asian Americans greater visibility and representation on screen.

Moreover, independent cinema has also been influential in shaping the way we consume and interact with films. The rise of streaming services has democratized the film industry, making it easier for independent filmmakers to distribute their work to a wider audience. Platforms such as Netflix, Amazon Prime, and Hulu have enabled independent films to reach audiences worldwide, providing greater exposure to filmmakers who might otherwise struggle to secure a theatrical release.

In conclusion, independent cinema has had a profound impact on culture and society, giving voice to marginalized communities, challenging societal norms, and sparking important conversations and debates. Independent films have also been instrumental in promoting diversity and inclusion in the film industry and have been influential in shaping the way we consume and interact with films. As the film industry continues to evolve, independent cinema will undoubtedly play a vital role in shaping its future, and we can expect to see more groundbreaking and thought-provoking films in the years to come.

The world of independent cinema is constantly evolving, and as technology and distribution methods continue to change, so too does the potential for growth and success in the industry. In this final section, we will explore the potential for future growth and success in independent cinema.

First and foremost, it is important to recognize that independent cinema has already achieved a significant level of success. Over the past few decades, independent films have gained recognition and acclaim from audiences and critics alike, and have even been able to compete with big-budget Hollywood productions at the box office and in awards shows.

One of the factors contributing to this success has been the advent of new technologies and distribution methods. Digital technology has made it easier and more affordable for independent filmmakers to produce high-quality films, and the rise of streaming services has given these films a broader and more accessible audience than ever before. With the ability to reach viewers around the world, independent filmmakers now have the opportunity to connect with a global audience and build a following that can lead to further success.

Another important factor contributing to the potential for future growth in independent cinema is the increasing demand for diverse and authentic stories. As audiences become more conscious of representation and inclusion in media, there is a growing appetite for films that reflect a broader range of experiences and perspectives. Independent filmmakers are uniquely positioned to tell these stories, as they are often able to take risks and explore topics that may not be considered mainstream or commercially viable by larger studios.

However, there are also challenges facing the independent cinema industry. One of the biggest challenges is the increasingly crowded and competitive marketplace. With so many films being produced and distributed each year, it can be difficult for independent filmmakers to stand out and attract attention. This is especially true given the high cost of marketing and advertising in the film industry, which can make it difficult for smaller productions to compete with larger studios.

Another challenge facing independent filmmakers is the ongoing struggle for funding. While digital technology has made it easier and more affordable to produce films, it is still a costly and risky venture. Independent filmmakers often rely on grants, loans, and crowdfunding to finance their productions, which can be a difficult and time-consuming process.

Despite these challenges, there are many reasons to be optimistic about the future of independent cinema. As audiences become more diverse and demanding, there is a growing appetite for films that tell unique and authentic stories. With the ability to reach a global audience through streaming services and other digital platforms, independent filmmakers now have the opportunity to connect with viewers around the world and build a following that can lead to further success.

Ultimately, the potential for future growth and success in independent cinema will depend on the ability of filmmakers, distributors, and audiences to adapt to new technologies and changing market conditions. As the industry continues to evolve, it will be important for independent filmmakers to stay agile and innovative, finding new ways to tell compelling stories and reach a wider audience. With the right combination of talent, creativity, and perseverance, there is no doubt that independent cinema will continue to thrive in the years to come.

THE END

To help you better understand the language and concepts related to aging and older adults, below you will find a list of key terms and their definitions.

Key terms

1. Independent cinema - A form of cinema that is produced outside of the mainstream film industry, often with lower budgets and creative freedom.

2. Auteur - A filmmaker who has a personal creative vision and signature style that is recognizable in their films.

3. Sundance Film Festival - A renowned film festival that takes place annually in Utah, USA, and is known for showcasing independent films.

4. Distribution - The process of making a film available to audiences through various channels, such as theatrical releases, streaming platforms, or physical media.

5. Financing - The process of securing funds to cover the costs of producing a film, which can come from various sources such as investors, grants, or crowdfunding.

6. Film festivals - Events that showcase and celebrate films from different genres, countries, and formats, often providing opportunities for networking, promotion, and recognition.

7. Genre - A category or type of film that is defined by its themes, motifs, and conventions, such as comedy, drama, horror, or documentary.

8. Box office - The amount of money a film earns from ticket sales during its theatrical run.

9. Blockbuster - A highly successful and popular film that attracts large audiences and generates significant revenue.

10. Streaming services - Platforms that allow viewers to stream movies and TV shows over the internet, such as Netflix, Amazon Prime Video, or Hulu.

Supporting Materials

Introduction:

- Rosenbaum, J. (2002). Essential cinema: On the necessity of film canons. The Johns Hopkins University Press.

Chapter 1: The Independent Filmmaker:

- Biskind, P. (1999). Easy riders, raging bulls: How the sex-drugs-and-rock 'n' roll generation saved Hollywood. Simon & Schuster.

- Levy, E. (2011). Cinema of outsiders: The rise of American independent film. NYU Press.

Chapter 2: The Sundance Film Festival:

- Cooper, P. M. (2005). Sundance: A festival virgin's guide: Surviving and thriving at America's most important film festival. Watson-Guptill Publications.

- Fuhrmann, W. (2010). The Sundance Kid: A biography of Robert Redford. W. W. Norton & Company.

Chapter 3: Iconic Independent Films of the Late 80s:

- James, D. (2008). The most typical avant-garde: History and geography of minor cinemas in Los Angeles. University of California Press.

- Schatz, T. (1998). The new Hollywood. Da Capo Press.

Chapter 4: Funding and Distribution in Independent Cinema:

- Balio, T. (1985). The American film industry. University of Wisconsin Press.
- De Valck, M. (2017). Film festivals: From European geopolitics to global cinephilia. Amsterdam University Press.
Chapter 5: The Impact of Independent Cinema on Hollywood:
- Leonard, G. (2010). Cinema, culture and Hollywood's war on terror. I.B. Tauris.
- Neale, S. (2000). Genre and contemporary Hollywood. British Film Institute.
Chapter 6: The Future of Independent Cinema:
- Dovey, J. (2015). Film and female consciousness: Irigaray, cinema and thinking women. Palgrave Macmillan.
- Hjort, M., & Petrie, D. (Eds.). (2007). The cinema of small nations. Edinburgh University Press.
Conclusion:
- King, G. (2016). American independent cinema. Routledge.
- Rosenbaum, J. (2014). Goodbye cinema, hello cinephilia: Film culture in transition. University of Chicago Press.

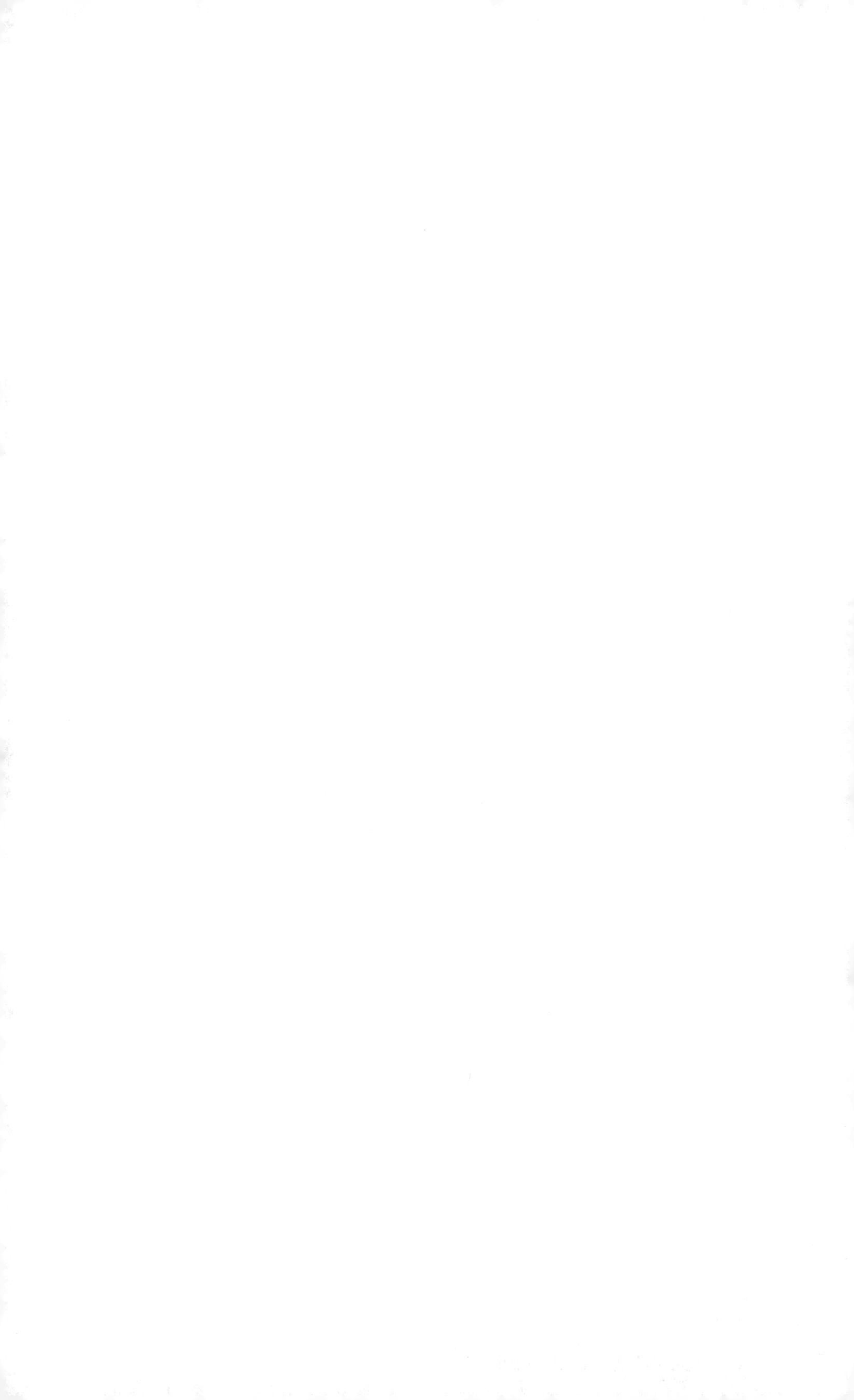